Introduction

Every day many people around the world throw away things they don't want. So much is being thrown away it has become a problem for us and for the planet. People have to work out ways to make less rubbish.

The good news is there are many ways that the amount of rubbish can be reduced. This book tells you how people are working to **reduce**, **reuse** and **recycle** rubbish and how you can help to reduce rubbish too.

Chapter 1

What's the problem with rubbish?

Think about ...

Think about what you've thrown away the past couple of days. What could you do to reduce the rubbish you make?

Are you the problem?

Are you throwing out more than you need to? Do you throw away things just because you want to replace them with something new? People love to get new things, but many of the new things we buy and the old things we throw away cause problems for the environment.

The packaging that our new things come in also causes problems. Most new things are sold in bags, wrappers, packets or boxes, which you throw away as soon as you get home.

We are running out of the **resources** that we need to make new things. That's why we have to think more about how we use resources.

We have to **reduce** our waste, and **reuse** and **recycle** things like wood, paper, clothing, wool, metals, glass, plastics and rubber.

Our space is limited

The whole world faces the problem of what to do with all the rubbish we make. Where does all the rubbish go? We send the rubbish to **landfills** where it is buried in the ground. But the landfills are filling up.

Landfills

Mariana is an environmental project manager for her local town council. It is her job to work out how the council can take care of the town's rubbish. She also helps to turn old landfills into parks. These are the questions she is asked most frequently.

Did you know?

Every year, the average Australian family produces enough rubbish to fill a three-bedroom house. Each day, they throw away about 2.25 kilograms of waste.

Q. **What are landfills?**

A. Landfills are places where rubbish is taken to be buried. Modern landfills are carefully prepared to prevent the chemicals from the rubbish leaking out.

Q. **What's in a landfill?**

A. Landfills are made up of just about anything people have thrown away. Food scraps, plants, plastic bags, papers, furniture, clothes, old tyres and other car parts can all be found in a landfill.

Q. **What happens to the rubbish when it gets to the landfill?**

A. First the rubbish is crushed so it takes up as little space as possible. Then it is put into the area, called a cell, where the rubbish for that day is going. At the end of the day the cell is covered in soil and crushed again.

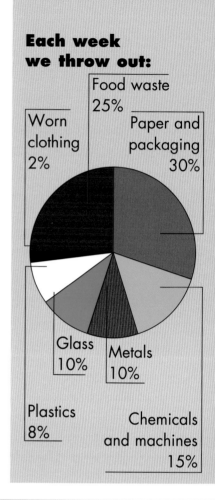

Each week we throw out:

- Food waste 25%
- Worn clothing 2%
- Paper and packaging 30%
- Glass 10%
- Metals 10%
- Plastics 8%
- Chemicals and machines 15%

A landfill site

Vent to take away gases. Some of the gas can be burned to make electricity.

Pump

New rubbish

Old rubbish

Soil
Drainage layer
Gravel
Liner
Clay

Drain to take away toxic water

Q. What happens to the rubbish that is buried in landfills?

A. Landfills are designed to be as dry and airless as possible. This means that very little of the rubbish **decomposes**. So it stays where it is!

Q. What happens when the landfill becomes full?

A. It is covered with a plastic sheet and more soil. Plants like grass are planted on the area. Trees are not planted as their roots may penetrate the plastic sheet as they grow. Sometimes the landfills are made into parks or golf courses after they have been covered.

Think about ...

Why do you think landfills are dry and airless?

Trucks arriving with rubbish at a landfill site

Q. **Why are landfills a problem?**

A. Because people make a lot of rubbish, landfills take a lot of space. Even when rubbish is crushed, a landfill gets used up quickly. Also, things in landfills stay there forever. It would be better for the planet if the waste that is going to landfills could be recycled in some way.

Q. **What can we do to help?**

A. The best thing we can do is not make rubbish. The next thing we can do is reuse and recycle as much of our rubbish as possible.

Did you know?

After a landfill closes, it must be **monitored** for 30 years or more to make sure it is not leaking toxic chemicals into the environment.

Our resources are limited

The world has a limited amount of natural resources like wood, metal and oil. A resource like metal is never replenished. Once we have mined all the metal, there will be no new metal left in the ground.

Some natural resources can be replenished but it takes a very long time. Trees are like this. They take a short time to cut down, but it takes many years for new trees to grow. We are in danger of using trees more quickly than they can grow.

Another problem is that metal and wood go into landfills instead of being reused and recycled. This is something we all have the power to change.

Chapter 2

People taking action

While we still have a lot of work to do to save the environment, many people are doing amazing things to help. They have thought of many ways to **reduce, reuse** and **recycle** things like wood, paper, clothing, wool, metal, glass, plastic and rubber.

Reduce

The best way to save **resources** is to avoid using things you don't have to use. This might mean riding your bike instead of taking a ride in a car. It could mean making sure your pens are all used up before you buy new ones. Or it could even mean not buying something new that you want but don't really need.

People can reduce waste by saving resources, too. People put out things they no longer need for the local council to collect and recycle. These things can be old furniture or shelving, and bicycles or toys that children no longer use. In this way, there are less things going to landfill.

Some community groups organise a goods exchange weekend. Websites such as Freecycle and Ziilch are set up for people to exchange secondhand goods. If anyone wants your things, they send you an email. Then you choose who you give your things to.

? Did you know?

To reduce plastic waste the weight of two-litre plastic soft drink bottles has dropped to 50 grams per bottle. About 30 years ago, the weight of the same sized bottle was 68 grams. That means about 113 million kilograms of plastic per year has not been made into bottles, and as a result, has not become rubbish. The bottles can be recycled after they are used as well.

Almost 50 per cent of all the truck and bus tyres in Britain are retreads. About 90 per cent of all the tyres on aircraft are retreads too. Reusing all those tyres saves natural resources and saves space in **landfills**. Find out more about how tyres are made and how old tyres are recycled.

Activity

Have a look at the pictures to find tyres used in a new way. Can you think of any other ways to use tyres apart from on wheels?

Reuse

Reusing means using something again. It is possible to reuse things in two different ways. You can reuse things by repairing or cleaning them to make them as good as new. Or, you can find a new way to use something.

Reusing tyres

Every day in Britain over 100,000 worn rubber tyres are taken off cars, vans and trucks. This equals about 40 million tyres every year. Imagine if all those tyres went straight to a landfill. Fortunately 70 per cent of these tyres are reused or recycled. They are inspected to make sure they are strong enough to be reused, and a new surface is put on them to repair them. These tyres are called retreads.

Zoo composting

Some zoos recycle all the waste from particular plant-eating animals such as elephants and giraffes.

The Melbourne Zoo, in Australia, tries to reduce, recycle or reuse materials in as many ways as it can. The zoo uses a machine called Hot Rot to convert organic waste, such as animal manure, grass, leftover food and compostable packaging into garden fertiliser. The fertiliser is sold in nurseries for people to use in their gardens.

The Detroit Zoo, in Michigan, USA, produces zoo waste for use on urban farms and community gardens. The zoo has plans to use an airtight container called an anaerobic digester to produce renewable energy. It will turn the methane gas from the zoo waste into electricity. This electricity will be used to power the zoo's animal hospital, which will save the zoo $80,000 each year in energy costs.

The Oregon Zoo, in the USA, **composts** 1,200 cubic metres of manure. When this big pile becomes hot, it reduces to 890 cubic metres of compost. People can come to the zoo and collect the compost for their gardens.

Recycle

Recycling is more complicated than reducing or reusing, because it usually involves changing the recycled rubbish back into a raw material, then using the raw material to make something new.

Recycling rubber

Tyres that are not safe to retread can be recycled. They can be used as fuel to make electricity. In California the electricity generated from burning tyres is used to power 3,500 homes. Tyres are also shredded so their rubber can be reused.

Recycling glass

About 10 per cent of everything we throw away is made of glass. A lot of this glass can be recycled and made into new glass containers.

Recycling metals

Many metals can be recycled. Do you ever wonder what happens to drink cans after you put them out to be recycled? Many cans are recycled with other objects made of aluminium.

Recycling plastic

Did you know that you may be wearing recycled rubbish right now? If you are wearing any polar fleece clothing, it may once have been a plastic bottle. It doesn't feel like a plastic bottle, and it certainly doesn't look like one, but it really is made out of the same material.

Plant Waste Recycler

Don't throw your garden waste away! Save on landfill costs and let us take it to our composting plant! No plant is too big or too small! Grass cuttings, weeds, hedge clippings and trees can be turned into compost. We can also take away extra soil and rocks to be recycled.

Clean up your garden and help us help the environment!

CALL US TODAY!
800-COMPOST

Find out more

All plant matter will rot and turn into soil. This releases **nutrients** back into the earth so that other plants can absorb them. This helps other plants to grow up healthy and strong. Find out more about how to make compost.

CLOTHES! CLOTHES! CLOTHES!

Is your wardrobe bursting at the seams? Have you got clothes you haven't worn for years? Call us to collect them so they can be reused or recycled. Clothes in good condition can be given to those in need, here and in other countries. Worn-out clothes can be recycled and their **fibres** reused, so you will help the environment. Not only will needy people thank you, so will the planet...

Let us help you get rid of the clutter and help those in need! Call us at 800-FIBRESAVE now!

Australians send more than half a million tonnes of clothes, shoes and bags to landfill each year. We could help to reduce this waste by buying fewer clothes and recycling more.

Chapter 3

What can you do?

There are many things you can do to help the environment. It may seem that the problem is too big for you to do much, but if everyone does something small, it will make a big difference.

At home: Inside

Megan's family decided that it was time they started to take better care of the environment.

They worked out what they could **reduce**.

WE CAN REDUCE

Batteries   Buy rechargable batteries, so we don't have to throw away used ones.

Packaging   Try to avoid buying things with a lot of packaging that goes straight in the rubbish.

Shopping   Take bags that we can reuse.

Paint   When we redecorate we will plan what we need so we don't waste and throw away paint.

Compost   Put our **food waste** into Mum's compost for the garden.

They worked out what they could **reuse**.

WE CAN REUSE

<u>Glass and plastic containers</u>
Store food, pens and other things we might reuse in art projects.

<u>Clothes</u>
Give away Megan's and Tom's old clothes they've outgrown – get the children recycled clothes from their cousins. (Lucky they're cool!)

<u>Keep</u>
Interesting worn-out clothes for Dad's quilt project.

They worked out what they could **recycle**.

WE CAN RECYCLE

cans

plastic bottles

glass

paper

cardboard

worn-out clothes

towels, bedsheets, blankets

Think about ...
Think about the ways you could make your house more environmentally friendly. Compare this with what you read in this chapter.

Recycling might sound like hard work, but it is easy once you try. And it is a great feeling to help make the world a cleaner place.

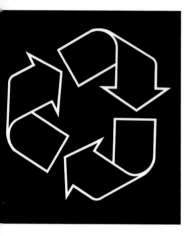

At home: Outside

The chart on the next page shows you some things that your parents will be able to recycle if they have a garden or garage. Things in the green boxes can be recycled into a compost heap. Other things will have to be taken to a recycling centre to be recycled by experts.

Whether or not you have a garden of your own, you can help to make the outdoors a cleaner, greener place. There will be a community project with a centre near you. These projects organise big cleanup days as well as teaching people how they can all make a difference by recycling rubbish. They help communities to make plans for their areas and they help teachers tell you about what you can do for your community.

Find out more

Find out more about volunteering to help clean up your area. The Keep Australia Beautiful website at *kab.org.au* will tell you all you need to know.

Things you can recycle from outdoors

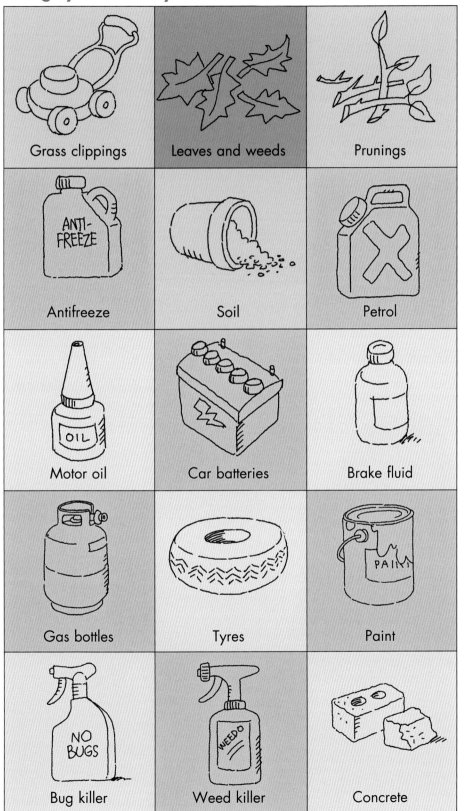

Grass clippings	Leaves and weeds	Prunings
Antifreeze	Soil	Petrol
Motor oil	Car batteries	Brake fluid
Gas bottles	Tyres	Paint
Bug killer	Weed killer	Concrete

Your parents might be able to recycle these things from outside the house and in the garden. Many chemicals have to be recycled by people who know how to handle chemicals safely, at a recycling centre. Sometimes the chemical and its container can both be recycled!

Did you know?

Eco-Schools is a program to help schools become more environmentally friendly. If your school is an Eco-School it can link to other Eco-Schools around the world at *eco-schools.org.au* to share environmentally friendly ideas.

Think about ...

If you take your lunch to school, you can use a plastic box rather than paper or plastic wrap. This helps the environment, as a plastic container can be washed and reused many times. What else can you do at your school to help the environment?

At school

The things you do at home to care for the planet can be done at school too. If your school doesn't have a recycling program, ask if your class can figure out how the school can recycle. You may be able to get special rubbish bins to recycle items like cans and plastic bottles. You may be allowed to set up a compost heap with your teacher or a caretaker to recycle food waste and create a school garden.

Reduce at school

At Neisha and Gilda's school the students and teachers have made a great effort to reduce waste and recycle more. When they get new stationery supplies they ask for products with as little packaging as possible. They make sure they use up all their notebook paper before they buy new books. They take good care of their art supplies to make sure nothing is wasted.

But their biggest success is what happens to food scraps at school. The food waste is recycled.

Food scraps go to the compost bin.

In the compost bin, the scraps turn into fertiliser.

The vegetables are used for making healthy meals at home or school.

Fertiliser from the compost bin goes onto the school vegetable garden.

The plants use the **nutrients** in the compost to grow.

CORN

CORN

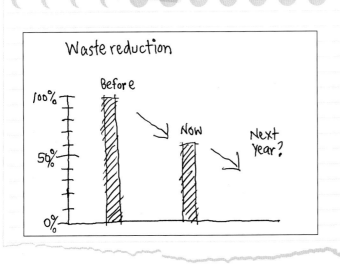

Waste reduction

100%

50%

0%

Before

Now

Next year?

At Neisha and Gilda's school they are thinking of ways to do even better.

Limiting waste

As the population of the world grows, so does the amount of rubbish we make. What we do with waste really matters. Some people are taking action. People are thinking up new ways to recycle and reuse lots of things. Now you know how you can help!

Reduce, reuse, recycle!

Think about ...

Think about what you could make from rubbish.

Glossary

compost a rubbish heap of plant matter

decompose to break down naturally in the environment

fibre fine threadlike pieces of a material

landfill a place where rubbish is buried

monitor to watch carefully

nutrients nourishment that helps plants grow

recycle processing old things so their materials can be made into new things

reduce to make or use less

resources a supply of materials or energy

reuse to use something again or more than once

Index